Teacher's Reso[...]
Number and Operations-Fractions

Daily Common Core Review

Reteaching

Practice

Enrichment

Scott Foresman·Addison Wesley

enVisionMATH®
Common Core

PEARSON

Glenview, Illinois • Boston, Massachusetts • Chandler, Arizona • Upper Saddle River, New Jersey

PEARSON

ISBN-13: 978-0-328-68787-9
ISBN-10: 0-328-68787-1

 **Domain**
Number and Operations - Fractions

Topic 9	**Understanding Fractions**
Topic 10	**Fraction Comparison and Equivalence**

Each lesson has a Teacher Resource Master for Daily Common Core Review, Reteaching, Practice and Enrichment.

Topic 9 Understanding Fractions

Topic 10 Fraction Comparison and Equivalence

Name _____

Choose the best answer.

1. Sara has 28 books. If she has the same number of books on each of 4 shelves, how many books are on each shelf?

   A 5

   B 6

   C 7

   D 8

2. What is another way of thinking of 4×8?

   A $(2 \times 8) + (2 \times 8)$

   B $(2 \times 4) + (2 \times 4)$

   C $(2 \times 2) + (4 \times 4)$

   D $(3 \times 4) + (3 \times 4)$

3. Leon has 6 cousins. He wants to give them each 8 pieces of chewing gum. How many pieces of chewing gum does Leon need?

   A 48

   B 36

   C 14

   D 2

4. Which list shows the numbers from greatest to least?

   A 738, 745, 726

   B 745, 738, 726

   C 745, 726, 738

   D 726, 738, 745

5. **Mental Math** It takes Don 45 minutes to finish his math homework and 25 minutes to finish his reading homework. How many more minutes did Don spend on his math homework than on his reading homework?

   _____

6. What are the next two items in the pattern below?

   A6, B7, C8, _____, _____

7. Roger's score on a computer game is 709 points. Greg's score is 438 points. How many more points did Roger score than Greg?

   _____

8. Write a fact family with 3, 6, and 18.

   _____

   _____

D 9·1

Dividing Regions into Equal Parts

A whole can be divided into equal parts in different ways.

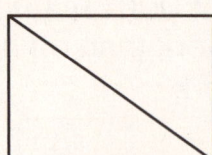

2 equal parts
halves

3 equal parts
thirds

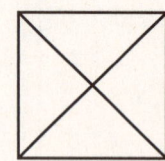

4 equal parts
fourths

5 equal parts
fifths

6 equal parts
sixths

8 equal parts
eighths

10 equal parts
tenths

12 equal parts
twelfths

Tell if each shows equal parts or unequal parts.
If the parts are equal, name them.

1.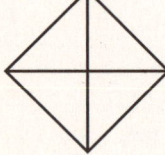

_____

2.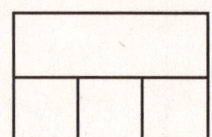

_____

3.

_____

Name the equal parts of the whole.

4.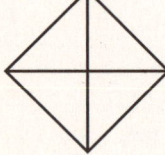

_____

5.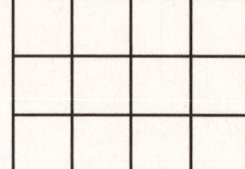

_____

6.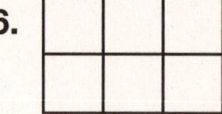

_____

7. Using grid paper, draw a picture of a whole that is divided into thirds.

8. Reason How many equal parts are there when you divide a figure into fifths? _____

Dividing Regions into Equal Parts

Tell if each shows equal or unequal parts.
If the parts are equal, name them.

1.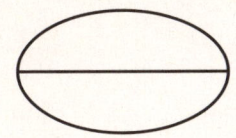

_____

_____

2.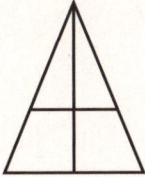

_____

_____

3.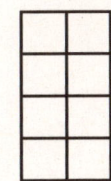

_____

_____

4.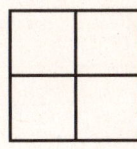

_____

_____

Name the equal parts of the whole.

5.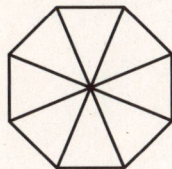

_____

6.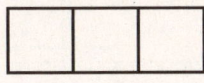

_____

7.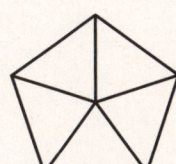

_____

8.

_____

Use the grid to draw a region showing the number of equal parts named.

9. eighths

10. sixths

11. How many equal parts does this figure have?

_____

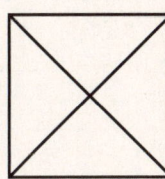

12. Which is the name of 12 equal parts of a whole?

    A halves   **B** sixths   **C** tenths   **D** twelfths

It's All the Same

A square with a side of 4 ft needs to be cut into four shapes with the same area. Can you find six different ways to cut the square? Draw six different ways the square could be cut on the squares below.

1.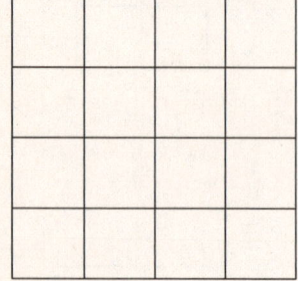

2.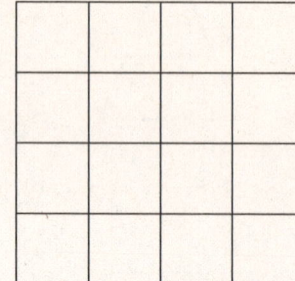

3.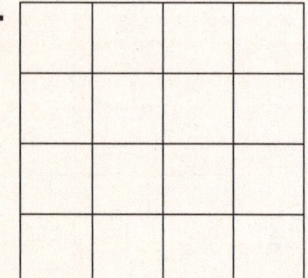

4.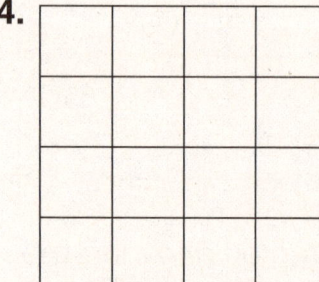

5.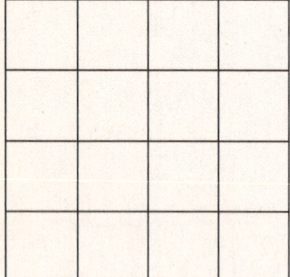

6.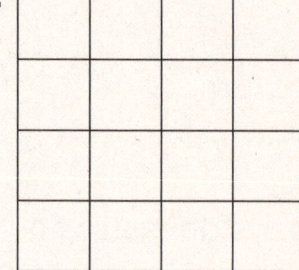

Name _____

Choose the best answer.

1. Which of the problems below has a quotient of 6?

   A 42 ÷ 6   **C** 48 ÷ 8

   B 35 ÷ 7   **D** 63 ÷ 9

2. Pedro needs three times as many onions as peppers for his stew. If he needs 9 peppers, how many onions does he need?

   A 27   **C** 6

   B 12   **D** 3

3. Which shape is shown below?

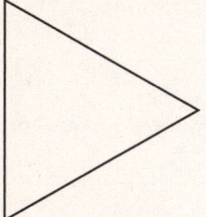

   A Triangle   **C** Rectangle

   B Square   **D** Pentagon

4. Estimation Patrick has 142 baseball cards. Gene has 528 baseball cards. Which is the best estimate for how many more cards Gene has than Patrick?

   A 670   **C** 390

   B 590   **D** 300

5. What is the greatest product of a 1-digit number multiplied by a 1-digit number? Write the multiplication sentence you used.

_____

Use the chart below to answer **6** and **7**.

Birds at the Feeder in 1 Hr	Tally	Number
Cardinals	|||	3
Chickadees	ⵌ	5
Blue Jays	|	1
Goldfinches	||	2
Sparrows	ⵌ ||||	9

6. How many more chickadees were at the feeder than cardinals?

_____

7. How many more sparrows were there than cardinals?

_____

8. Write a fact family with 6, 9, and 54.

_____

_____

Fractions and Regions

A fraction can be used to name part of a whole.

A unit fraction is a fraction with a numerator of 1.

The denominator shows the total number of equal parts in a whole.

The numerator shows how many equal parts are described.

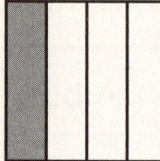

| number of parts shaded $\longrightarrow$ | <u>1</u> | $\longleftarrow$ Numerator |
| number of equal parts $\longrightarrow$ | 4 | $\longleftarrow$ Denominator |

One fourth of the rectangle is shaded.

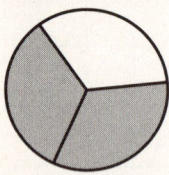

Each part of   There are 2 $\frac{2}{3}$ of the whole
the circle is $\frac{1}{3}$.   parts shaded.   circle is shaded.

In **1–4,** write the unit fraction that represents each part of the whole. Write the number of shaded parts and the fraction of the whole that is shaded.

1.

2.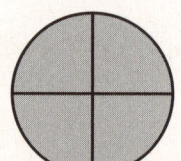

3.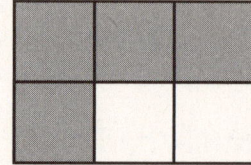

4.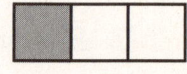

_____   _____   _____   _____

5. Draw a rectangle that shows 2 equal parts. Shade $\frac{1}{2}$ of the rectangle.

6. Draw a circle that shows 4 equal parts. Shade $\frac{3}{4}$ of the circle.

Fractions and Regions

In 1–4, write the unit fraction that represents each part of the whole. Write the number of shaded parts and the fraction of the whole that is shaded.

1.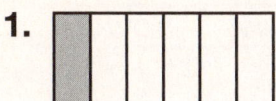

2.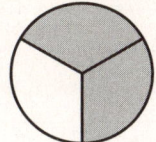

3.

4.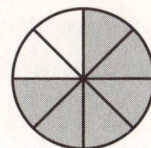

_____   _____   _____   _____

5. Draw a circle that shows 4 equal parts. Shade $\frac{2}{4}$ of the circle.

6. Draw a hexagon that shows 6 equal parts. Shade $\frac{4}{6}$ of the hexagon.

In 7 and 8, use the information below.

Three parts of a rectangle are red. Two parts are blue.

7. What fraction of the rectangle is red?

8. **Reason** What fraction of the rectangle is blue?

_____   _____

9. **Model** A banner is made of 8 equal parts. Five of the parts contain stars. Three of the parts contain hearts. Draw the banner.

10. How can you write the fraction $\frac{4}{6}$ in word form?

    A fourth sixth   **B** four sixes   **C** four sixths   **D** fourth six

What's in a Word?

Words are made up of both consonants and vowels, and all letters are either consonants or vowels. *Y* may be used as a vowel in some cases. In the following, let *y* be used only as a consonant.

1. Complete the table by writing a fraction for the number of consonants and a fraction for the number of vowels in each word. The first one has been done for you.

Word	Consonants	Vowels
Trombone	$\frac{5}{8}$	$\frac{3}{8}$
Label		
International		
Porpoise		
Success		
World		
Apology		
Language		

2. Complete the table by writing a word that fits the fraction of consonants and the fraction of vowels shown. The first one has been done for you.

Word	Consonants	Vowels
Visit	$\frac{3}{5}$	$\frac{2}{5}$
	$\frac{2}{4}$	$\frac{2}{4}$
	$\frac{4}{7}$	$\frac{3}{7}$
	$\frac{3}{6}$	$\frac{3}{6}$
	$\frac{5}{8}$	$\frac{3}{8}$
	$\frac{3}{4}$	$\frac{1}{4}$
	$\frac{2}{5}$	$\frac{3}{5}$
	$\frac{2}{3}$	$\frac{1}{3}$

Name _____

Choose the best answer.

1. What fraction of the figure below is shaded?

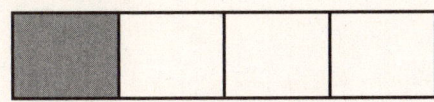

A $\frac{3}{4}$ C $\frac{1}{3}$

B $\frac{2}{3}$ D $\frac{1}{4}$

2. Which number sentence is part of the same fact family as $28 \div 7$?

A $4 \times 7 = 28$ C $28 - 4 = 24$

B $4 + 7 = 11$ D $28 + 4 = 32$

3. Which number makes the number sentence true?

$4 \times 10 = \blacksquare \times 4$

A 40   C 10

B 14   D 6

4. Rosa puts 9 hammers into 3 toolboxes.

Which number sentence shows how many hammers are in each toolbox?

A $9 + 3 = 12$ C $9 \div 3 = 3$

B $9 \times 3 = 12$ D $9 - 3 = 6$

5. Draw a figure that shows $\frac{3}{4}$.

6. Compare the expressions. Use <, >, or =.

$9 \times 2 \bigcirc 3 \times 8$

7. Estimation Sammy is playing a board game with Jose. Sammy scores 327 points and Jose scores 442 points. About how many points did Jose win?

_____

8. Write the name of the polygon shown below.

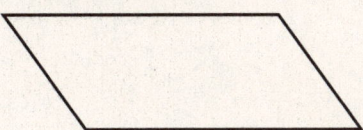

_____

9. Find the quotient.

$17 \div 1 =$ _____

Fractions and Sets

A fraction can name part of a group.

What fraction of the marbles are black?

 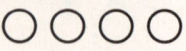
$\dfrac{3}{8}$ ← Number of black marbles

← Total number of marbles

$\dfrac{3}{8}$ of the marbles are black.

---

1. What fraction of the toys are balls? _____

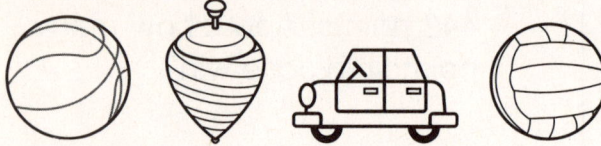

2. What fraction of the fruits are oranges? _____

3. What fraction of the blocks have letters on them? _____

4. What fraction of the letters in the word Monday is *M*? _____

For **5** and **6** draw a picture to show each fraction of a set.

5. $\dfrac{3}{6}$ of the squares are shaded.

6. $\dfrac{2}{3}$ of the balls are footballs.

7. **Reason** Out of 6 cats, 2 are tan. What fraction of cats are **NOT** tan? _____

Fractions and Sets

In **1** through **3**, write the fraction of the counters that are shaded.

1.

_____

2.

_____

3.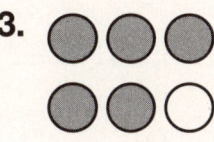

_____

Draw a picture of the set described.

4. 4 shapes, $\frac{3}{4}$ of the shapes are squares

5. 6 shapes, $\frac{1}{6}$ of the shapes are circles

6. 8 shapes, $\frac{7}{8}$ of the shapes are triangles

In **7** and **8**, use the utensils to answer the questions.

7. What fraction of the utensils are forks?

_____

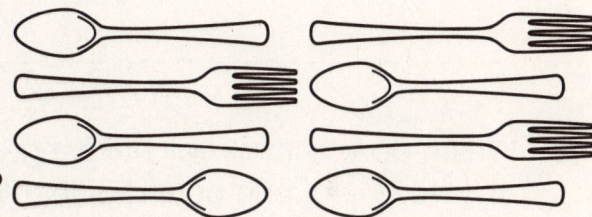

8. What fraction of the utensils are spoons?

_____

9. Persevere Johnny bought 6 movie tickets and spent $54. Of the tickets he bought, $\frac{3}{6}$ were children's tickets that cost $8 each. The other tickets were adult tickets. How much does one adult ticket cost?

_____

10. Pamela has 4 pink ribbons, 3 green ribbons, and 1 blue ribbon. What fraction of Pamela's ribbons are green?

A $\frac{1}{3}$ **B** $\frac{3}{8}$ **C** $\frac{2}{3}$ **D** $\frac{3}{4}$

Choices

1. Would you rather have $\frac{1}{2}$ of 22 pennies or $\frac{1}{3}$ of 3 dimes?
   Explain.

   _____

   _____

   _____

   _____

2. Would you rather have $\frac{1}{4}$ of a 16 oz drink or $\frac{1}{2}$ of an 8 oz drink? Explain.

   _____

   _____

   _____

   _____

3. Which do you think will have a greater value, $\frac{1}{8}$ of one pound
   of gold or $\frac{1}{4}$ of one pound of lead? Why?

   _____

   _____

   _____

   _____

4. Jane needs to miss fewer than $\frac{1}{6}$ of the words on her spelling
   list. If there are 18 words, how many can she miss? Explain.

   _____

   _____

   _____

Name _____

Choose the best answer.

1. There are 8 dogs at the park.
Three of the dogs are poodles,
2 are huskies, and 3 are terriers.
What fraction of the dogs
are poodles?

  A $\frac{2}{8}$

  B $\frac{3}{8}$

  C $\frac{4}{8}$

  D $\frac{5}{8}$

2. Which statement is true about
all parallelograms?

  A They have 4 right angles.

  B They have 5 sides.

  C They have only one pair of
parallel sides.

  D Opposite sides are parallel.

3. **Mental Math** The dancers on the
stage are standing in rows. There
are 21 dancers in row one. There
are 19 dancers in row two. How
many dancers are on the stage?

  A 30

  B 39

  C 40

  D 50

4. Which is the next number in the
pattern below?

57 49 41 33 25

  A 34

  B 24

  C 17

  D 7

5. The line plot shows days with 0, 1,
2, or 3 inches of rainfall.

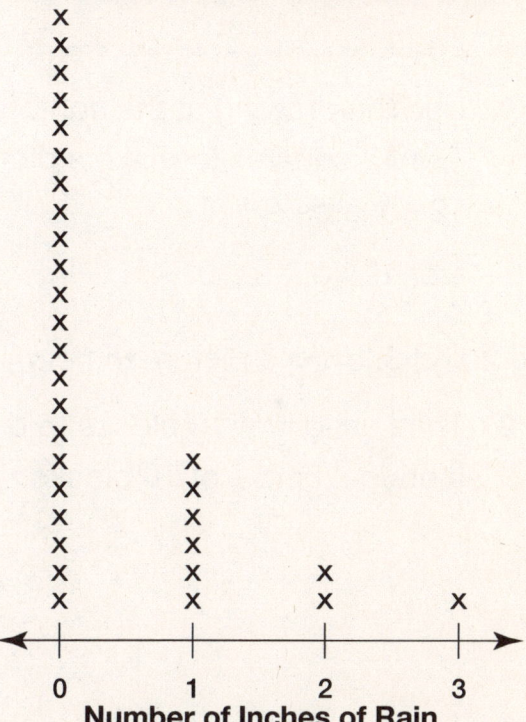

Fort Myers Daily Rainfall in July

Number of Inches of Rain

How many days had only 1 inch
of rain?

_____

Fractional Parts of a Set

You can find how many there are in a fraction of a set.

Find $\frac{1}{3}$ of 15 triangles.

First look at the denominator of the fraction.

$\frac{1}{3}$ ← 3 equal parts in all

So, put 15 triangles into **3** equal groups.

 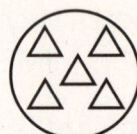 

Next, look at the numerator of the fraction.

$\frac{1}{3}$ ← 1 of the equal parts

So, find how many triangles are in 1 of the equal parts.

 There are 5 triangles.
$\frac{1}{3}$ of 15 = 5

---

1. Use the drawing at the right. Morris used $\frac{1}{4}$ of 12 squares to make a picture. Find $\frac{1}{4}$ of 12 squares.

   $\frac{1}{4}$ of 12 = _____

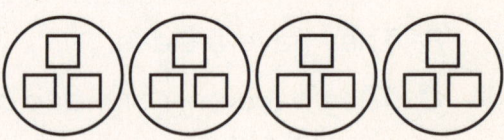

   Morris used _____ squares.

In **2** and **3,** draw a picture to help.

2. Thea used $\frac{1}{2}$ of 10 blocks to build a house. Find $\frac{1}{2}$ of 10 blocks.

3. Nate used $\frac{1}{8}$ of 24 crayons to draw a picture. Find $\frac{1}{8}$ of 24.

   $\frac{1}{2}$ of 10 = _____

   Thea used _____ blocks.

   $\frac{1}{8}$ of 24 = _____

   Nate used _____ crayons.

4. **Writing to Explain** When you divide 24 by 6, what fraction of 24 are you finding? Find the answer.

   _____

   _____

Name _____

Fractional Parts of a Set

1. Luann read $\frac{1}{3}$ of 18 books on her reading list. How many books did Luann read? Find $\frac{1}{3}$ of 18 books.

2. Jake used $\frac{1}{6}$ of 30 pencils in a pack. How many pencils did Jake use? Find $\frac{1}{6}$ of 30 pencils.

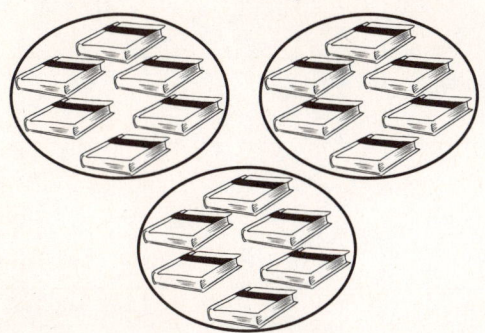

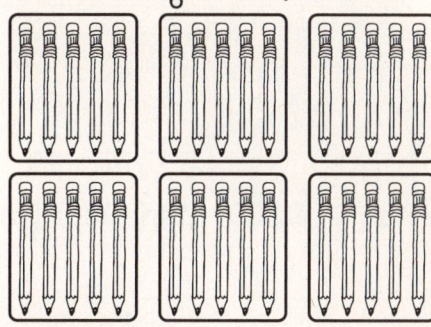

$\frac{1}{3}$ of 18 = _____

$\frac{1}{6}$ of 30 = _____

Luann read _____ books.

Jake used _____ pencils.

3. There are 12 eggs in a carton. Kim used $\frac{1}{3}$ of a carton of eggs to make muffins. How many eggs did she use? Explain how you found your answer.

_____

_____

_____

4. **Model** Draw a picture in the space at the right to show how you would find $\frac{1}{2}$ of 8 marbles.

5. What number represents $\frac{1}{8}$ of 24 students?

   A 2   **B** 3   **C** 4   **D** 8

Money Amounts

For **1–6**, decide which person has more money.
Explain how you chose.

1. Jon has $\frac{2}{3}$ of $12. Kate has $\frac{3}{4}$ of $12.

_____

_____

2. Ann has $\frac{1}{6}$ of $30. Maria has $\frac{1}{3}$ of $30.

_____

_____

3. Sara has $\frac{2}{4}$ of $20. Marco has $\frac{1}{2}$ of $20.

_____

_____

4. Ben has $\frac{1}{4}$ of $16. Paulo has $\frac{2}{8}$ of $16.

_____

_____

5. Gary has $\frac{1}{2}$ of $18. Erin has $\frac{2}{3}$ of $18.

_____

_____

6. Kari has $\frac{4}{6}$ of $24. Julie has $\frac{2}{3}$ of $24.

_____

_____

7. What does your answer to Exercise 6 tell you about the
fractions $\frac{4}{6}$ and $\frac{2}{3}$?

_____

_____

Name _____

Choose the best answer.

1. Which is the missing number on the number line below?

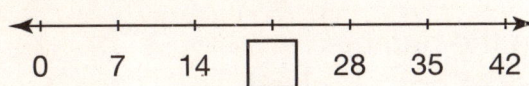

0   7   14   ☐   28   35   42

A 17

B 21

C 23

D 25

2. Roger has 715 points on a computer game. Greg has 438 points. How many more points does Roger have than Greg?

A 277

B 377

C 407

D 437

3. **Mental Math** What is the difference of 152 − 42?

A 100

B 110

C   98

D   86

4. What fraction of the circles are shaded?

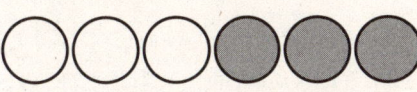

A $\frac{6}{3}$

B $\frac{6}{6}$

C $\frac{3}{6}$

D $\frac{2}{6}$

5. The table below shows the total number of wheels needed for the different numbers of trucks at Jim's Truck Company. Complete the table.

Number of Trucks	Total Number of Wheels Needed
1	6
3	18
6	36
7	

Explain how you found your answer.

_____

_____

_____

Locating Fractions on the Number Line

Number lines can be used to show fractions. In the number lines below, the denominator shows the number of equally sized sections between 0 and 1.

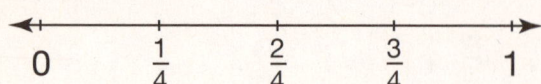

This number line is divided into fourths.

This number line is divided into sixths.

Number lines can also represent mixed numbers.

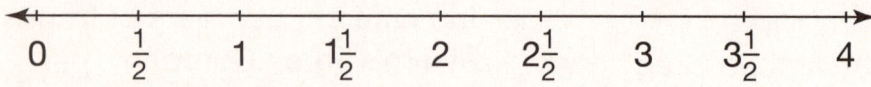

This number line is divided into halves.

Write the missing fraction or mixed number for each number line.

1.

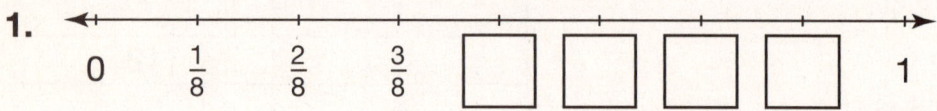

2.

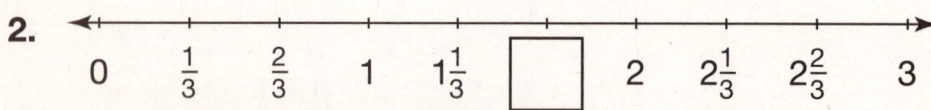

3.

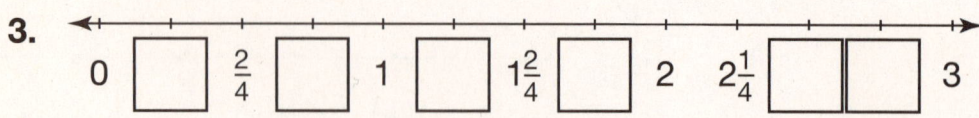

4. Construct Arguments Erica said that $1\frac{3}{4}$ is between 2 and 3 on a number line. Do you agree? Why or why not?

_____

_____

Locating Fractions on the Number Line

Write the missing fraction or mixed number for each number line.

1.

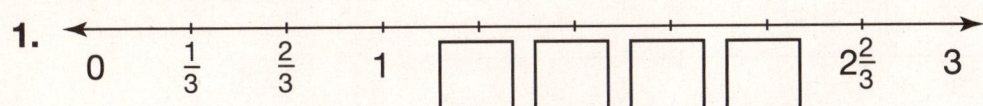

2.

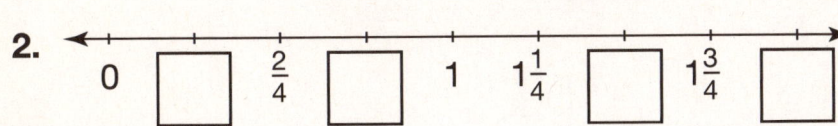

The number line below shows how many miles different places are from the pet shop. Use the number line for **3–5**.

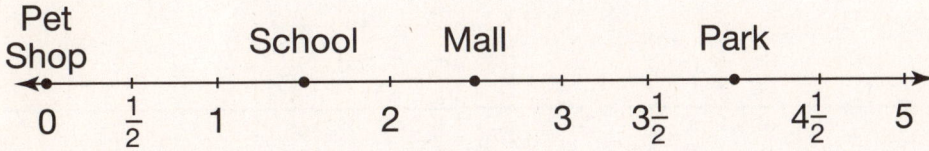

3. The park is 4 miles from the pet shop. How far is the mall from the pet shop?

_____

4. **Reason** Ken lives halfway between the pet shop and the park. How far does Ken live from school?

_____

5. The movie theater is twice as far from the school as the mall. If the movie theater is to the right of the school, at which location is the movie theater?

_____

6. Roberta is going to make a number line from 0 to 4 by $\frac{1}{4}$s. Not including the mark for 0, how many marks should she draw?

A 8   **B** 12   **C** 16   **D** 20

What's in a Name?

Each point on a number line has more than one name.
Write some of the names for each point on the number line.

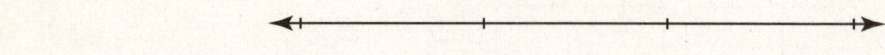

Label fourths. $\frac{1}{4}$ _____   _____   _____

Label halves.   _____   _____

Label whole
numbers.   _____

Label fourths. $\frac{4}{4}$ _____ $\frac{6}{4}$ _____   _____

Label halves. $\frac{2}{2}$ _____   _____

Label whole   1 $1\frac{1}{4}$ _____   _____   _____
or mixed numbers.

Label fourths. $\frac{8}{4}$ _____ $\frac{10}{4}$ _____   _____

Label halves. $\frac{4}{2}$ _____   _____

Label whole   2   _____   _____   _____
or mixed numbers.

Choose the best answer.

1. Lan bought the three bags of marbles shown below. How many marbles did Lan buy in all?

   A 6

   B 10

   C 15

   D 18

2. Which number makes the number sentence below true?

   $\square \div 6 = 8$

   A 48

   B 36

   C 24

   D 12

3. Two square tables are placed end to end to form one longer table. What shape is formed by the longer table?

   A Rectangle

   B Square

   C Hexagon

   D Octagon

4. **Estimation** Gila Cliff Dwellings National Monument has an area of 533 acres. Oregon Caves National Monument has an area of 488 acres. About how many acres larger is Gila Cliff Dwellings than Oregon Caves?

   _____

5. An acre is 43,560 square feet. What is the value of the 3 in 43,560?

   _____

6. Solve the following equation.

   $n \times 5 = 35$

   _____

7. Name the polygon shown below.

   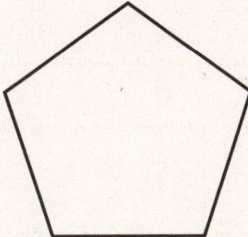

   _____

8. What is the name of a triangle with three equal sides?

   _____

Benchmark Fractions

You can use benchmark fractions to help you estimate parts.
Benchmark fractions are $\frac{1}{4}$, $\frac{1}{3}$, $\frac{1}{2}$, $\frac{2}{3}$, and $\frac{3}{4}$.

One way to think of benchmark fractions is to think of part of a clock.

$\frac{1}{2}$ shaded $\frac{1}{3}$ shaded $\frac{2}{3}$ shaded

$\frac{1}{4}$ shaded $\frac{3}{4}$ shaded

Estimate the fractional part that is shaded.

1.

_____

2.

_____

3.

_____

4.

_____

5. Number Sense About how much of the casserole is left over?

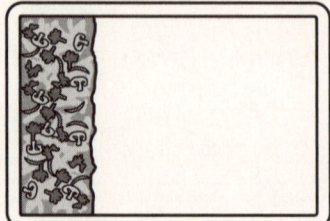

_____

Benchmark Fractions

Estimate the fractional part of each strip that is shaded.

1.

_____

2.

_____

3.

_____

4.

_____

What benchmark fraction is closest to each point? Choose from the benchmark fractions $\frac{1}{2}$, $\frac{1}{3}$, $\frac{2}{3}$, $\frac{1}{4}$, and $\frac{3}{4}$.

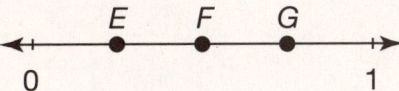

5. E _____

6. F _____

7. G _____

Estimate the amount that is left.

8.

9.

10.

_____

11. Model Draw a circle and shade it to show about $\frac{1}{3}$ shaded.

12. Which is the best estimate for the amount of the square that is shaded?

A $\frac{1}{4}$ **C** $\frac{1}{2}$

B $\frac{1}{3}$ **D** $\frac{2}{3}$

Fill the Cups

Match each drawing to the fraction that each
figure represents.

1. $\frac{2}{3}$ _____

A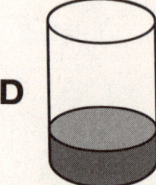

2. $\frac{1}{4}$ _____

B

3. $\frac{1}{2}$ _____

C

4. $\frac{3}{4}$ _____

D

5. $\frac{1}{3}$ _____

E

6. Write the fractions in order from least to greatest.

_____

Choose the best answer.

1. Which fact does **NOT** belong in the same fact family as the others?

   A $2 \times 8 = 16$

   B $16 \div 2 = 8$

   C $8 + 2 = 10$

   D $8 \times 2 = 16$

2. There are 1 actor and 3 actresses in the play that Cheyenne is going to see. What fraction of the performers are actors?

   A $\frac{3}{4}$

   B $\frac{2}{4}$

   C $\frac{1}{4}$

   D $\frac{1}{8}$

3. **Mental Math** Madison earned $55 for dog-sitting Ms. Alvarez's dog. Then she earned $26 for doing household jobs for Mrs. Jenkins. How much money did Madison earn in all?

   A $81

   B $91

   C $100

   D $101

4. Draw a figure that shows $\frac{3}{8}$.

5. What is the least number that rounds to 80 when rounded to the nearest ten?

   _____

6. Using the numbers 3, 7, 4, and 5, make the greatest 4-digit number and the least 4-digit number. Use each digit once.

   _____

7. Write a division sentence that can be used to represent the following repeated subtraction.

   $24 - 8 = 16$
   $16 - 8 = 8$
   $8 - 8 = 0$

   _____

Fractions and Length

A fraction can name part of the length of an object.

What part of this line segment is black?

You can use fraction strips to find the part of the whole.

$\frac{1}{4}$	$\frac{1}{4}$	$\frac{1}{4}$	$\frac{1}{4}$

The line segment is $\frac{3}{4}$ black. The line segment is $\frac{1}{4}$ gray.

What fraction of the length of the 1 strip do the other strips show?

1. | 1 |

| $\frac{1}{4}$ |

_____

2. | 1 |

| $\frac{1}{6}$ | $\frac{1}{6}$ | $\frac{1}{6}$ | $\frac{1}{6}$ |

_____

3. | 1 |

| $\frac{1}{8}$ | $\frac{1}{8}$ |

_____

4. | 1 |

| $\frac{1}{3}$ | $\frac{1}{3}$ |

_____

5. What fraction of the line segment is black? _____

| $\frac{1}{8}$ | $\frac{1}{8}$ | $\frac{1}{8}$ | $\frac{1}{8}$ | $\frac{1}{8}$ | $\frac{1}{8}$ | $\frac{1}{8}$ | $\frac{1}{8}$ |

6. Reason A figure is part blue and part red.

It is $\frac{5}{8}$ red. What part of the figure is blue? _____

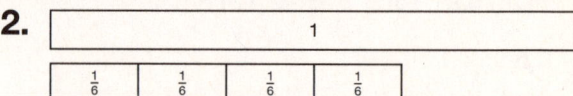
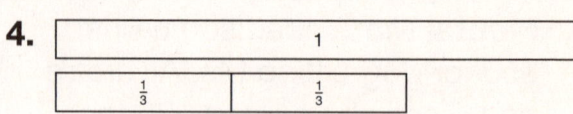

Name _____

Practice
9-7

Fractions and Length

What fraction of the length of the 1 strip do the other strips show?

1.

1

$\frac{1}{3}$

_____

2.

1

$\frac{1}{4}$	$\frac{1}{4}$	$\frac{1}{4}$

_____

3.

1

$\frac{1}{8}$	$\frac{1}{8}$	$\frac{1}{8}$	$\frac{1}{8}$	$\frac{1}{8}$

_____

4.

1

$\frac{1}{6}$	$\frac{1}{6}$	$\frac{1}{6}$	$\frac{1}{6}$

_____

In **5** and **6**, what fraction of each length of yarn is black?

5.

$\frac{1}{3}$	$\frac{1}{3}$	$\frac{1}{3}$

_____

6.

$\frac{1}{2}$	$\frac{1}{2}$

_____

7. Writing to Explain What is the purpose of using fraction strips and a 1 strip?

_____

_____

_____

_____

8. About $\frac{6}{8}$ of Earth's surface is covered by water. About what fraction of Earth's surface is not covered by water?

A $\frac{5}{8}$

B $\frac{1}{2}$

C $\frac{3}{8}$

D $\frac{2}{8}$

Find the Fraction!

Find the fraction of each set that is described.
Draw a picture to help. The first one has been done for you.

1. Matt has 10 toy trucks. Eight are blue. The rest
   are red.
   a. What fraction of the trucks are red?

   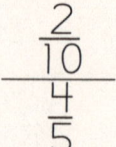

   b. How many fifths of the trucks are blue?

 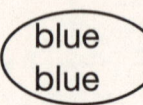  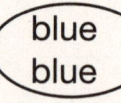 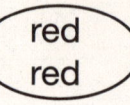

2. Amos cut 12 shapes out of paper. Three of the
   shapes are triangles. The other shapes are squares.
   a. What fraction of the shapes are triangles? _____

   b. How many fourths of the shapes are triangles? _____

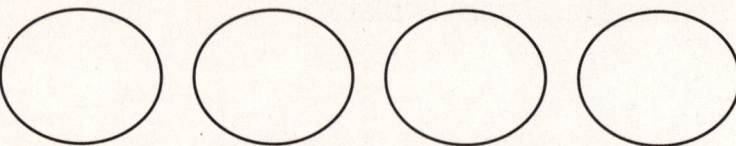

3. Jess has 8 stickers. Six of them are stars.
   The rest are smiley faces.
   a. What fraction of the stickers are stars? _____

   b. How many fourths of the stickers are stars? _____

4. Kelly has a board that is 6 feet long. She painted
   2 feet of the board green. The rest of the board
   is painted blue.
   a. What fraction of the board is green? _____

   b. How many thirds of the board are painted green? _____

Choose the best answer.

1. The slide costs $1. The Ferris wheel costs $2. Stephen and Alicia went on each ride the same number of times. Together, they spent $12 in all. How many times were they on each ride?

   A 2

   B 3

   C 4

   D 5

2. Juanita wants to buy a computer that costs $779. She also wants to buy a printer that costs $136. How much money will Juanita spend all together?

   A $925

   B $915

   C $905

   D $805

3. Which of the following fractions is a unit fraction?

   A $\frac{2}{3}$

   B $\frac{5}{8}$

   C $\frac{1}{8}$

   D $\frac{4}{8}$

4. Write a multiplication and division fact family using 7, 9, and another number.

   _____

   _____

5. What is the next number in the pattern below?

   27, 35, 43, 51, 59, _____

6. Draw a picture of a circle with 6 equal parts.

   What fraction represents each part of the circle?

   _____

7. Find the product.

   $2 \times 3 \times 5$ _____

8. **Estimation** Find the estimate of 739 + 195.

   _____

Problem Solving: Make a Table and Look for a Pattern

Unger Soda hired 20 testers to try their new celery soda. Seven of the testers did not like the taste of the new soda. Suppose that pattern continues. If 100 people were hired in all, how many would **NOT** like the taste of the soda?

Make a table. Then write the information that you know. Find a pattern to extend the table until you find the results for 100 testers.

Doesn't Like	7	14	21	28	35	Increases by 7.
Total Testers	20	40	60	80	100	Increases by 20.

So, 35 people out of 100 will not like the taste of the Unger's celery soda.

Complete each table to solve.

1. Ms. Lee is buying bags of mixed dumplings. There are 40 dumplings in each bag. In each bag are 10 pork dumplings. If Ms. Lee buys 200 dumplings, how many will be pork dumplings?

Pork Dumplings	10				
Total Dumplings	40				

2. Packages of mixed socks contain 8 pairs of socks. In each package, there are 5 pairs of white socks. How many pairs of white socks would there be in 40 pairs of socks?

Pairs of White Socks	5				
Total Pairs of Socks	8				

3. **Look for a Pattern** Look back at Exercise 2. What pattern do you see?

_____

_____

_____

4. **Write a Problem** Write a problem that can be solved by making a table and using a pattern. Then solve the problem.

_____

_____

_____

Problem Solving: Make a Table and Look for a Pattern

Complete each table to solve.

1. Roses at a flower shop are sold in packages of 6. Each package contains 4 red roses. How many red roses will you get if you buy 30 roses?

Red Roses	4				
Total Roses	6				

2. There are 20 lollipops in each package of Yum's Lollipops. Each package contains 4 grape lollipops. How many grape lollipops will you get if you buy 100 lollipops?

Grape Lollipops	4				
Total Lollipops	20				

3. There are 9 bottles of salsa in a gift pack of Pedro's Salsa. In each gift pack, 2 of the bottles are extra spicy. Suppose someone buys 45 bottles. How many of the bottles will be extra spicy?

Extra Spicy Bottles	2				
Total Bottles	9				

4. Reason Look back at Exercise 3. Suppose Jackie bought 27 bottles.

a. How many of the bottles would NOT be extra spicy?

_____

b. How many more bottles are not extra spicy than are extra spicy?

_____

5. In a package of 25 colored pencils, 8 are red. If you bought 125 pencils, how many would be red?

Red Pencils	8				
Total Pencils	25				

6. Write a Problem Write a problem that can be solved by making a table and using a pattern. Then solve the problem.

_____

_____

_____

Money Patterns

Complete each table. Then use it to solve each problem.

1. Diego is making the penny pattern shown below.
   He wants to make 5 rows. How much will all the pennies be worth?

Rows	1	2	3	4	5
Pennies	3	6	9		

   Answer: _____

2. Lauren is making the nickel pattern shown below.
   She wants to makes 4 rows. How much money will all the nickels be worth?

Rows	1	2	3	4
Nickels	5	7	9	

   Answer: _____

3. Doug is making the dime pattern shown below.
   He wants to makes 5 rows. How much money will all the dimes be worth?

Rows	1	2	3	4	5
Dimes	4	8	12		

   Answer: _____

Choose the best answer.

1. Ella made 215 large bookmarks to sell at a school fair. She made 95 small bookmarks. How many bookmarks in all did she make to sell at the fair?

   A 310

   B 300

   C 210

   D   20

2. What fraction is shown by the shaded parts below?

   A $\frac{3}{8}$

   B $\frac{4}{8}$

   C $\frac{3}{5}$

   D $\frac{5}{8}$

3. **Mental Math** There are 7 days in one week. How many days are in 8 weeks?

   A 15 days

   B 49 days

   C 56 days

   D 63 days

4. Karin made a bracelet of beads. For every 3 yellow beads in the bracelet, she used 1 blue bead. Her bracelet has 6 blue beads. How many yellow beads did Karin use?

   A 24

   B 18

   C 10

   D   3

5. Each weekday Ms. Long runs 5 miles. After 3 weeks, how far has she run?

   _____

6. Jared takes 75 shots in basketball practice on Monday. He takes 48 shots on Tuesday, and 83 on Wednesday. How many shots does he take in all three days?

   _____

Using Models to Compare Fractions: Same Denominator

You can use fraction strips to compare fractions with the same denominator.

Compare $\frac{2}{4}$ and $\frac{3}{4}$.

1		
$\frac{1}{4}$	$\frac{1}{4}$	
$\frac{1}{4}$	$\frac{1}{4}$	$\frac{1}{4}$

$\frac{2}{4}$ ◯ $\frac{3}{4}$

When fractions have the same denominator, the fraction with the *greater* numerator is greater.

Compare. Write >, <, or =.

1.

1			
$\frac{1}{8}$	$\frac{1}{8}$	$\frac{1}{8}$	$\frac{1}{8}$
$\frac{1}{8}$	$\frac{1}{8}$	$\frac{1}{8}$	$\frac{1}{8}$	$\frac{1}{8}$

$\frac{5}{8}$ ◯ $\frac{4}{8}$

2.

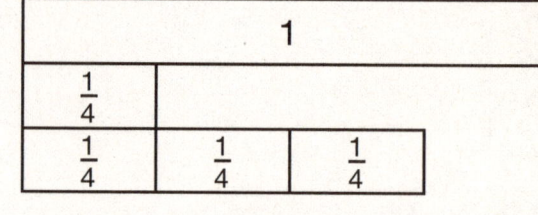

1		
$\frac{1}{4}$		
$\frac{1}{4}$	$\frac{1}{4}$	$\frac{1}{4}$

$\frac{1}{4}$ ◯ $\frac{3}{4}$

3. $\frac{5}{6}$ ◯ $\frac{2}{6}$

4. $\frac{2}{3}$ ◯ $\frac{1}{3}$

5. If two fractions have the same denominator but different numerators, which fraction is greater? Give an example.

_____

_____

_____

Using Models to Compare Fractions: Same Denominator

Compare. Write >, <, or =.

1.

	1	
$\frac{1}{6}$	$\frac{1}{6}$	$\frac{1}{6}$
$\frac{1}{6}$	$\frac{1}{6}$	

$\frac{3}{6}$ ◯ $\frac{2}{6}$

2.

	1	
$\frac{1}{3}$		
	$\frac{1}{3}$	$\frac{1}{3}$

$\frac{1}{3}$ ◯ $\frac{2}{3}$

3. $\frac{2}{4}$ ◯ $\frac{3}{4}$

4. $\frac{5}{6}$ ◯ $\frac{3}{6}$

5. $\frac{4}{6}$ ◯ $\frac{1}{6}$

6. $\frac{3}{8}$ ◯ $\frac{6}{8}$

7. Why is $\frac{6}{8}$ greater than $\frac{5}{8}$ but less than $\frac{7}{8}$?

_____

_____

_____

_____

8. Reasonableness Marty ate $\frac{4}{6}$ of his pizza and Luis ate $\frac{5}{6}$ of his pizza. Marty ate more pizza than Luis. How is that possible?

_____

_____

_____

_____

9. Two fractions have the same denominator. Which is the greater fraction: the fraction with the greater numerator or the lesser numerator?

_____

_____

10. Which is the greatest fraction?

   A $\frac{0}{4}$ 　　　 B $\frac{1}{4}$ 　　　 C $\frac{3}{4}$ 　　　 D $\frac{2}{4}$

Look-Alikes

Write the fraction from the box that shows the smaller part of
each group. You will not use all of the fractions.

Fraction Box	$\frac{3}{4}$	$\frac{4}{6}$	$\frac{1}{4}$	$\frac{3}{8}$	$\frac{5}{8}$
$\frac{1}{3}$	$\frac{6}{8}$	$\frac{5}{6}$	$\frac{1}{6}$	$\frac{2}{3}$	$\frac{2}{6}$	$\frac{2}{8}$

1. 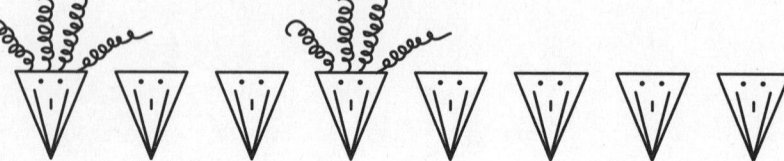 _____

2.  _____

3. 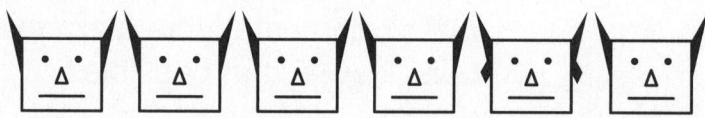 _____

4.  _____

5. 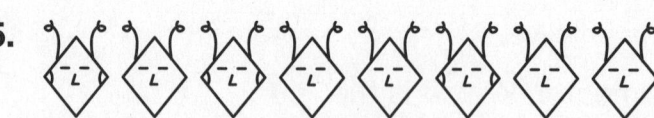 _____

6.  _____

7. Look at the fractions you did not use. Choose two with the same
denominator. Write a number sentence that compares them.

_____

Choose the best answer.

1. Which is the standard form of two hundred thousand, six hundred ninety-nine?

   A 269,600

   B 209,699

   C 206,690

   D 200,699

2. **Mental Math** Darren has 50 baseball cards and 23 football cards. What is the total number of cards Darren has?

   A 53

   B 55

   C 70

   D 73

3. There are 452 books in the children's reading room at the library. There are 509 books in the adult reading room. How many more books are there in the adult reading room than the children's reading room?

   A 47

   B 57

   C 67

   D 147

4. Which number has the greatest value?

   A 5,445

   B 4,455

   C 5,544

   D 4,554

Use the table for 5 through 8.

National Champion Trees	
Tree	**Height (in ft)**
Giant sequoia	275
Sugar pine	232
Coast Douglas fir	281
Port Orford cedar	219
Coast redwood	321

In 5–7, write a number sentence to compare the heights of the two trees. Use <, >, or =.

5. Giant sequoia and Coast redwood

6. Sugar pine and Port Orford cedar

7. Coast Douglas fir and Coast redwood

8. What is the height of a tree that has a greater height than a giant sequoia but less than a coast Douglas fir?

   _____ feet

Using Models to Compare Fractions: Same Numerator

You can compare fractions with the same numerator using fraction strips.

Compare $\frac{1}{3}$ and $\frac{1}{4}$.

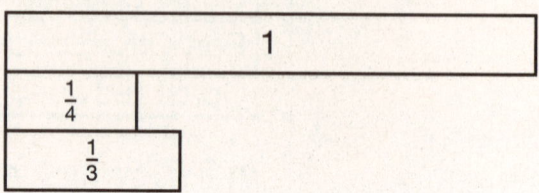

$$\frac{1}{3} \bigcirc \frac{1}{4}$$

When fractions have the same numerator, the fraction with the *lesser* denominator is greater.

Compare. Write <, >, or =.

1.

$$\frac{2}{8} \bigcirc \frac{2}{6}$$

2.

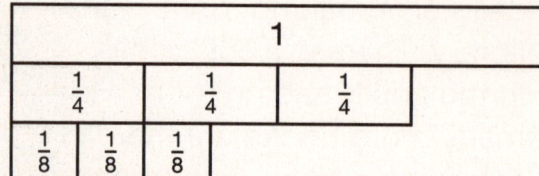

$$\frac{3}{4} \bigcirc \frac{3}{8}$$

3. $\frac{2}{3} \bigcirc \frac{2}{3}$

4. $\frac{3}{4} \bigcirc \frac{3}{6}$

5. Reason If two fractions have the same numerator but different denominators, which fraction is greater? Give an example.

_____

_____

_____

Using Models to Compare Fractions: Same Numerator

Compare. Write $<$, $>$, or $=$ for each $\bigcirc$.

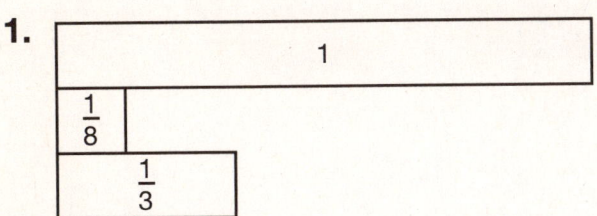

1.

	1	
$\frac{1}{8}$		
	$\frac{1}{3}$	

$\frac{1}{8} \bigcirc \frac{1}{3}$

2.

	1	
	$\frac{1}{3}$	$\frac{1}{3}$
$\frac{1}{6}$	$\frac{1}{6}$	

$\frac{2}{3} \bigcirc \frac{2}{6}$

3. $\frac{3}{6} \bigcirc \frac{3}{4}$

4. $\frac{1}{2} \bigcirc \frac{1}{2}$

5. $\frac{2}{8} \bigcirc \frac{2}{6}$

6. $\frac{3}{8} \bigcirc \frac{3}{4}$

7. Ricardo has read $\frac{2}{3}$ of a book. Lin had read $\frac{2}{4}$ of the same book. Who has read more of the book?

_____

8. Maria and Nina each ordered a small pizza. Maria ate $\frac{3}{8}$ of her pizza. Nina ate $\frac{3}{6}$ of her pizza. Who ate more pizza?

_____

9. Which is the greatest fraction?

A $\frac{1}{2}$ **B** $\frac{1}{4}$ **C** $\frac{1}{6}$ **D** $\frac{1}{8}$

10. Writing to Explain Why is $\frac{1}{6}$ greater than $\frac{1}{8}$ but less than $\frac{1}{3}$? Explain.

_____

_____

How Full?

Look at the shaded figures on the left and circle the figure
on the right that belongs in the same group.

1. 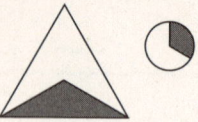   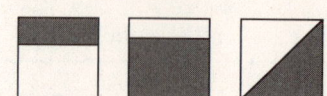

2. 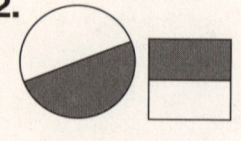   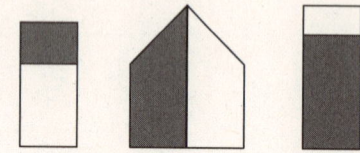

3. 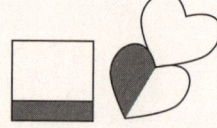   

4. 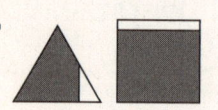   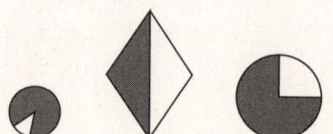

5. 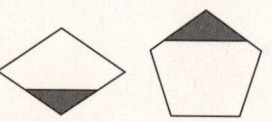   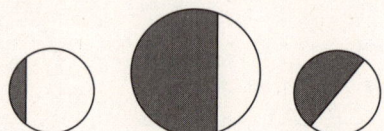

6. 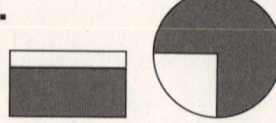   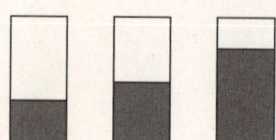

Choose the best answer.

1. 18 ÷ 3?

 A 2

 B 6

 C 8

 D 9

2. What fraction of the shape is shaded?

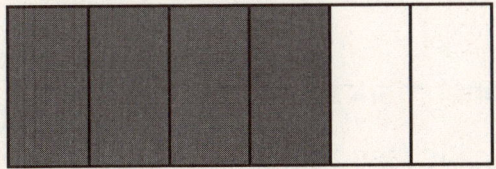

 A $\frac{2}{6}$

 B $\frac{2}{4}$

 C $\frac{4}{6}$

 D $\frac{6}{4}$

3. What is 312 rounded to the nearest ten?

 A 300

 B 310

 C 320

 D 400

4. Order the numbers from least to greatest.

961, 971, 917, 977

_____

_____

5. Estimation There are 276 students at Johnson Elementary School. There are 412 students at Eisenhower Elementary School. Estimate the total number of students all together.

_____

Use this information to answer **6** and **7.**

Phil has 10 golf balls. Steve has twice as many golf balls as Phil. Paul has 2 more golf balls than Phil and Steve have all together.

6. How many golf balls does Steve have?

_____

7. How many golf balls does Paul have?

_____

Comparing Fractions Using Benchmarks

In Ms. Adams' class, $\frac{2}{3}$ of students are wearing red and $\frac{2}{8}$ of students are wearing blue. She wants to know if more students are wearing red or blue.

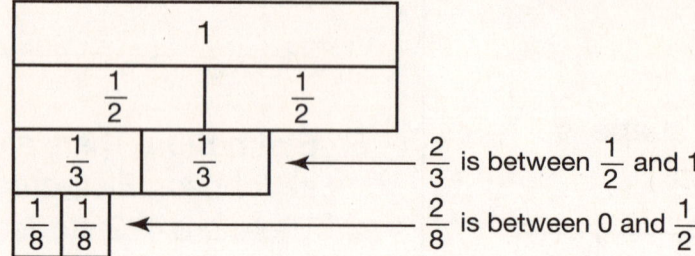

$\frac{2}{3}$ is between $\frac{1}{2}$ and 1

$\frac{2}{8}$ is between 0 and $\frac{1}{2}$

Ms. Adams can compare each fraction to the benchmark numbers 0, $\frac{1}{2}$, and 1.

$\frac{2}{3}$ is between $\frac{1}{2}$ and 1. $\frac{2}{8}$ is between 0 and $\frac{1}{2}$. So, $\frac{2}{8}$ is less than $\frac{2}{3}$.

More students in Ms. Adams' class are wearing red.

Mina, Bobby, and Julia each have the same number of pencils. $\frac{2}{6}$ of Mina's pencils are red, $\frac{2}{3}$ of Bobby's pencils are red, and $\frac{2}{4}$ of Julia's pencils are red.

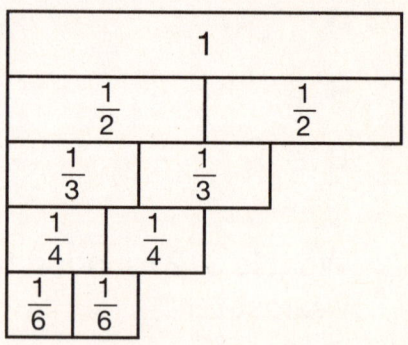

1. Who has more red pencils, Julia or Bobby?

   _____

2. Who has more red pencils, Mina or Julia?

   _____

3. **Reason** Which student has the most red pencils? Explain.

   _____

   _____

   _____

Name _____

Comparing Fractions Using Benchmarks

For **1–9**, use benchmark numbers to compare. Write < or > for each ◯.

1. $\frac{3}{6}$ ◯ $\frac{3}{8}$

2. $\frac{2}{3}$ ◯ $\frac{1}{3}$

3. $\frac{4}{8}$ ◯ $\frac{6}{8}$

4. $\frac{2}{4}$ ◯ $\frac{2}{6}$

5. $\frac{1}{4}$ ◯ $\frac{1}{3}$

6. $\frac{3}{4}$ ◯ $\frac{1}{4}$

7. $\frac{3}{3}$ ◯ $\frac{3}{4}$

8. $\frac{5}{8}$ ◯ $\frac{5}{6}$

9. $\frac{2}{6}$ ◯ $\frac{2}{3}$

10. Explain how you compared the fractions in Exercise 9.

_____

_____

11. Which fraction is closer to 1 than to 0?

   A $\frac{1}{4}$　　　　**B** $\frac{1}{2}$　　　　**C** $\frac{3}{6}$　　　　**D** $\frac{7}{8}$

12. Lucy has a collection of buttons. $\frac{2}{3}$ of her buttons are square and $\frac{2}{8}$ of her buttons are round. Does Lucy have more square buttons or round buttons?

_____

13. **Reason** On Monday, Carlos ran $\frac{1}{8}$ of a mile. On Wednesday, he ran $\frac{5}{6}$ of a mile. Carlos ran $\frac{3}{8}$ of a mile on Friday. Which day did Carlos run the farthest?

_____

14. **Writing to Explain** Sydney says that $\frac{4}{8}$ is closer to 0 than to 1. Is she correct? Explain.

_____

_____

_____

Comparing Fractions

Write each fraction to complete the chart.

U one fourth	_____
B four fourths	_____
O seven eighths	_____
P three eighths	_____
J three fourths	_____
E one half	_____
S one eighth	_____
R five eighths	_____

Write < or > to compare the value of each letter.

1. U _____ B   **2.** B _____ E   **3.** O _____ P

4. P _____ J   **5.** J _____ E   **6.** E _____ S

7. S _____ O   **8.** R _____ U   **9.** R _____ J

Write each letter from the chart in its correct spot on the number
line to find a hidden message.

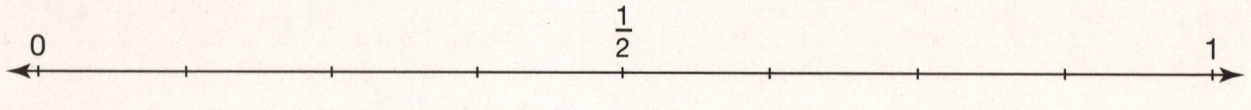

_____ _____ _____ _____ _____ _____ _____ _____

Name _____

Choose the best answer.

1. What fraction of the figure below is shaded?

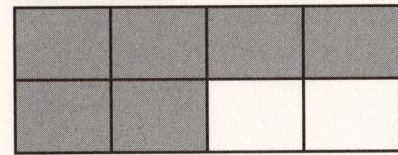

A $\frac{3}{8}$ C $\frac{5}{8}$

B $\frac{4}{8}$ D $\frac{6}{8}$

2. Louisa builds a kingdom of sandcastles at the beach. Her sandcastle kingdom is shown below.

Which number sentence could be used to find the total number of sandcastles in Louisa's kingdom?

A $4 \times 4 = \square$ C $4 - 4 = \square$

B $4 + 4 = \square$ D $4 \div 4 = \square$

3. Michael baked 54 cookies for his friends. He gave each of his 9 friends the same number of cookies. How many cookies did each friend get?

A 6   C 8

B 7   D 9

4. Fill in the missing number in the table below.

Normal Price	Sale Price
$15	$12
$21	$18
$27	$24
$40	

5. **Mental Math** There are 7 rows of chairs in the auditorium. Each row has 9 chairs. How many chairs are in the auditorium in all?

_____

6. Write the missing number.

$35,206 = 30,000 + \square + 200 + 6$

_____

Comparing Fractions on the Number Line

Yoko used a number line to compare $\frac{1}{4}$ and $\frac{3}{4}$.

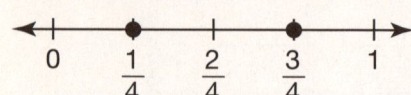

She marked where $\frac{1}{4}$ and $\frac{3}{4}$ are on the number line.
Then she looked for the fraction that was farther to the right.
She wrote $>$ to show which fraction is greater.

$\frac{3}{4}$ ◯ $\frac{1}{4}$

---

1. Mark $\frac{2}{3}$ and $\frac{1}{3}$ on the number line below.

   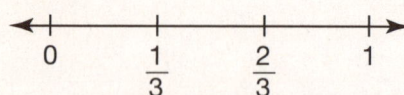

   Which fraction is greater, $\frac{2}{3}$ or $\frac{1}{3}$?
   Hint: It will be farther to the right.
   Write $>$ or $<$.

   $\frac{2}{3}$ ◯ $\frac{1}{3}$

2. Mark $\frac{1}{2}$ and $\frac{1}{6}$ on the number lines below.

   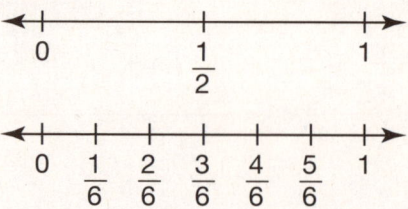

   Which fraction is greater, $\frac{1}{2}$ or $\frac{1}{6}$?
   Hint: It will be farther to the right.
   Write $>$ or $<$.

   $\frac{1}{2}$ ◯ $\frac{1}{6}$

3. **Use Structure** Simon is comparing $\frac{1}{3}$ yard and $\frac{2}{3}$ yard of rope.
   Circle the two denominators.

   $\frac{1}{3}$ ◯ $\frac{2}{3}$

   Since the denominators are the same, Simon can compare them
   on the same number line. Which number line should he use?

   A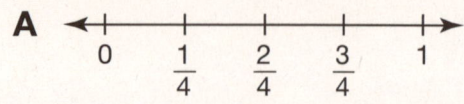

   B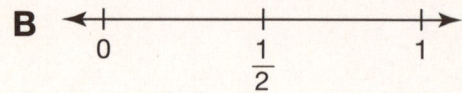

   C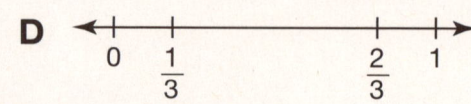

   D

Comparing Fractions on the Number Line

In **1–3,** compare. Write <, >, or =.
Draw number lines to help.

1. $\frac{3}{4}$ ◯ $\frac{1}{4}$

2. $\frac{2}{3}$ ◯ $\frac{1}{3}$

3. $\frac{6}{8}$ ◯ $\frac{7}{8}$

In **4–6,** compare. Write <, >, or =.
Draw number lines to help.

4. $\frac{1}{2}$ ◯ $\frac{1}{4}$

5. $\frac{2}{3}$ ◯ $\frac{2}{4}$

6. $\frac{1}{4}$ ◯ $\frac{1}{8}$

7. **Use Structure** When do you need to use two number lines to compare two fractions?

   A When you compare fractions that have the same denominators.

   B When you compare fractions that have different denominators.

   C When you compare fractions that are greater than 1.

   D When you compare fractions that refer to different wholes.

8. **Reason** Explain how you can use a number line to show that $\frac{5}{8}$ is greater than $\frac{3}{8}$.

   _____

   _____

   _____

Comparing Fractions on the Number Line

Solve each problem. Draw the number lines.
Find the greater fraction. Write > or <.

1.

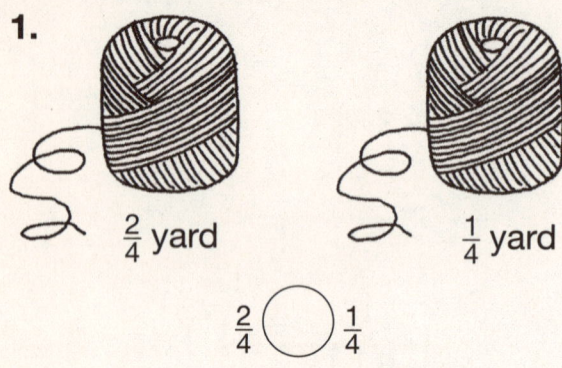

$\frac{2}{4}$ yard $\frac{1}{4}$ yard

$\frac{2}{4}$ ◯ $\frac{1}{4}$

2.

$\frac{3}{8}$ yard $\frac{5}{8}$ yard

$\frac{3}{8}$ ◯ $\frac{5}{8}$

3.

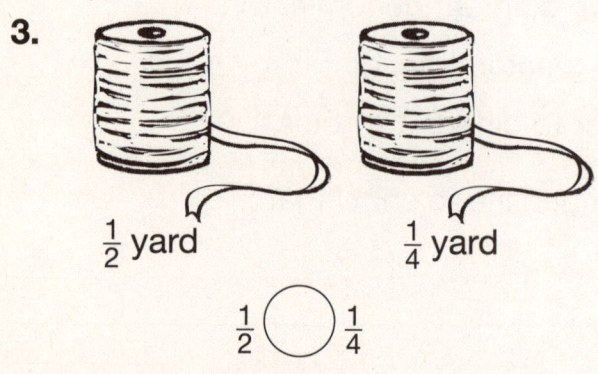

$\frac{1}{2}$ yard $\frac{1}{4}$ yard

$\frac{1}{2}$ ◯ $\frac{1}{4}$

4.

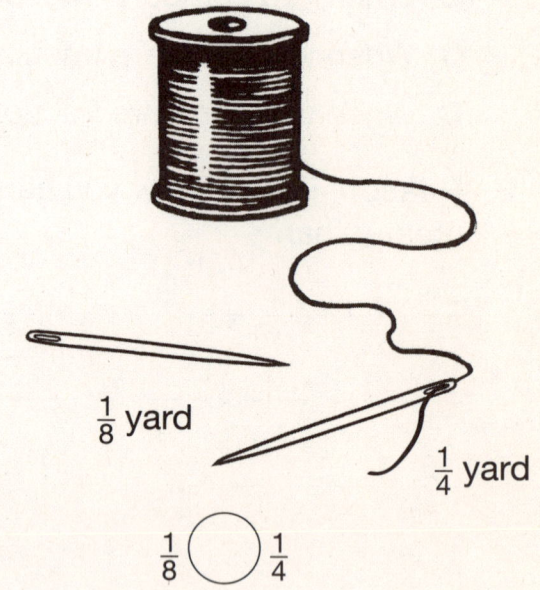

$\frac{1}{8}$ yard

$\frac{1}{4}$ yard

$\frac{1}{8}$ ◯ $\frac{1}{4}$

Name _____

Choose the best answer.

1. Which of these is the name for two lines that never intersect?

   A Circle   **C** Parallel Lines

   B Triangle   **D** Ray

2. What fraction is shown by the unshaded part in the figure below?

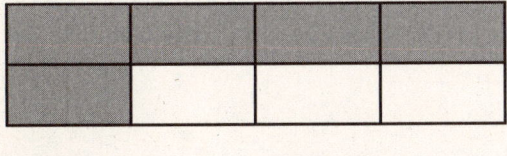

   A $\frac{2}{8}$ **C** $\frac{4}{8}$

   B $\frac{3}{8}$ **D** $\frac{5}{8}$

3. Mental Math A box of chocolates contains 8 chocolates. Sam bought 8 boxes of chocolate. How many chocolates does Sam have in all?

   A 56   **C** 72

   B 64   **D** 89

4. Karin made a bracelet of beads. For every 3 yellow beads in the bracelet, she used 1 blue bead. Her bracelet has 6 blue beads. How many beads did Karin use?

_____

5. Compare. Use $<$, $>$, or $=$.

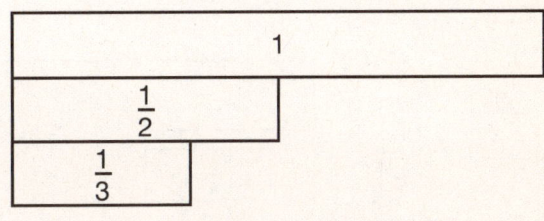

$\frac{1}{3}$ ◯ $\frac{1}{2}$

6. Brian's class has 3 fish tanks. The first tank contains 9 fish, the second has 11 fish, and the third has 13 fish. To make each fish tank have the same number of fish, what must Brian do?

_____

_____

7. Kevin earns $9 per hour. How much money does he earn on a day that he works 7 hours?

_____

Finding Equivalent Fractions

Equivalent fractions are fractions that name the same part of a whole. Equivalent fractions have different numerators and denominators, but their values are equal.

You can find equivalent fractions by using fraction strips.

$$\frac{1}{4} = \frac{\boxed{}}{8}$$

Find how many $\frac{1}{8}$s are equal to $\frac{1}{4}$. The denominator is 8 so use $\frac{1}{8}$ strips.

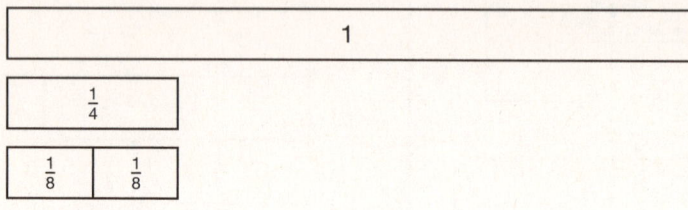

So, two $\frac{1}{8}$ strips are equal to $\frac{1}{4}$.

$$\frac{1}{4} = \frac{2}{8}$$

Another name for $\frac{1}{4}$ is $\frac{2}{8}$.

Complete each number sentence.

1.
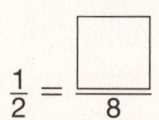

$$\frac{1}{2} = \frac{\boxed{}}{8}$$

2.
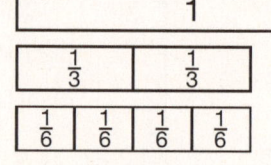

$$\frac{2}{3} = \frac{\boxed{}}{6}$$

3.
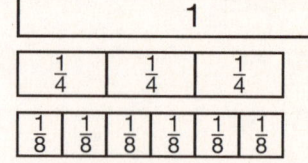

$$\frac{3}{4} = \frac{\boxed{}}{8}$$

4. Name two fractions that are equivalent to $\frac{1}{2}$.

_____

5. Reason Larry and Willa are each reading the same book. Larry has read $\frac{2}{3}$ of the book. Willa said that she has read more than Larry because she read $\frac{4}{6}$ of the book. Is Willa correct? Explain.

_____

_____

Finding Equivalent Fractions

Complete each number sentence.

1.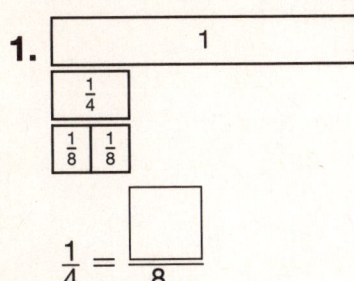

$\frac{1}{4} = \frac{\boxed{}}{8}$

2.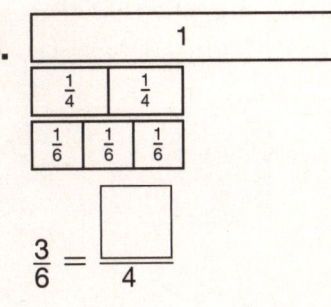

$\frac{3}{4} = \frac{\boxed{}}{8}$

3.

$\frac{3}{6} = \frac{\boxed{}}{4}$

Find the simplest form of each fraction.

4. $\frac{3}{6}$ _____

5. $\frac{4}{6}$ _____

6. $\frac{3}{8}$ _____

Name a fraction to solve each problem.

7. Rob colored $\frac{1}{4}$ of a rectangle. What is another way to name $\frac{1}{4}$?

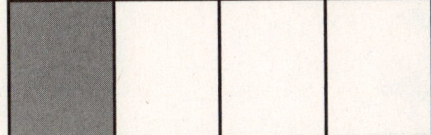

_____

8. Three eighths of the cast in a musical have to sing. What fraction of the cast does not have to sing?

_____

9. Use Tools When using fraction strips, how do you know that two fractions are equivalent?

_____

_____

_____

10. Samuel has read $\frac{3}{6}$ of his assignment. Judy has read $\frac{4}{8}$ of her assignment. Their assignments were the same size. Which sentence is true?

A Samuel read more than Judy.

B Judy read more than Samuel.

C They read the same amount.

D They will both finish the assignment at the same time.

Match Maker

Write the fraction that shows the shaded part. Then draw lines to match the shapes that show the equivalent fraction. The shapes can be different sizes, but must show equivalent fractions.

1.

_____

A.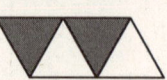

_____

2.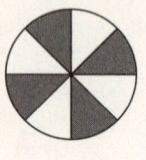

_____

B.

_____

3.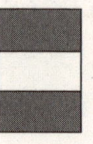

_____

C.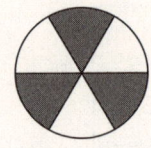

_____

4.

_____

D.

_____

5.

_____

E.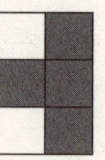

_____

6.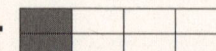

_____

F.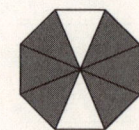

_____

Name _____

Choose the best answer.

1. **Estimation** Craig rode his bicycle
   32 miles on Monday, 58 miles on
   Wednesday, and 19 miles on Friday.
   What is the best estimate for the
   total number of miles Craig rode?

   A 90 miles

   B 100 miles

   C 105 miles

   D 110 miles

2. Which multiplication sentence
   shows this array?

   A $3 \times 3 = 9$

   B $3 \times 4 = 12$

   C $4 \times 3 = 12$

   D $4 \times 3 = 15$

3. Gwen received 3 baseball cards
   from each of her family members.
   She received a total of 12 cards.
   Which number describes how
   many family members gave
   Gwen cards?

   A 2

   B 4

   C 5

   D 6

4. Order the numbers from least to
   greatest.

   1,345, 1,356, 1,344

   _____

5. Write a fact family with 3, 7,
   and 21.

   _____

   _____

6. Mike had 4 boxes of crayons.
   Each box had 6 crayons. He gave
   all but 10 crayons to his friends.
   How many crayons did Mike give
   to his friends?

   _____

7. Find the product.

   $2 \times 3 \times 3$

   _____

Equivalent Fractions and the Number Line

Anna equally shares a bookshelf with her sister.
Her sister says Anna's books use $\frac{2}{4}$ of the shelf.
Anna thought her books used $\frac{1}{2}$ of the shelf.
Anna drew two number lines to see if the two numbers
are equivalent fractions.

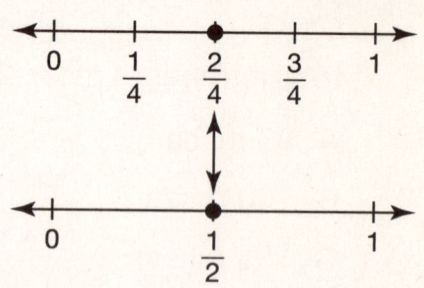

The fractions are at the same location on the number line.
The fractions are equivalent. $\frac{2}{4} = \frac{1}{2}$

For **1** and **2**, use the number lines given to complete the number
sentence.

1.
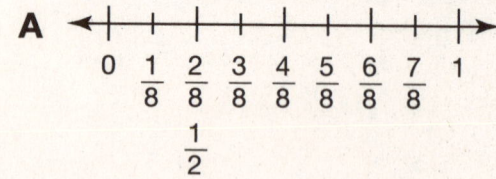

$\boxed{}$ $\frac{2}{3}$

$\frac{2}{6} = \boxed{}$

2.
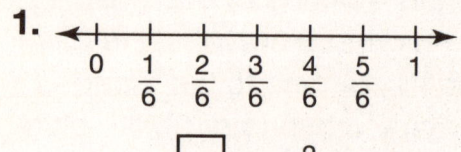

$\frac{1}{4}$ $\frac{2}{4}$ $\boxed{}$

$\frac{6}{8} = \boxed{}$

3. Reason Mick uses two pieces of rope to make ties for two cloth sacks.
One rope is $\frac{4}{8}$ yard. The other rope is $\frac{1}{2}$ yard. He wants to know if they
are the same length. Which number line correctly models the rope lengths?

A
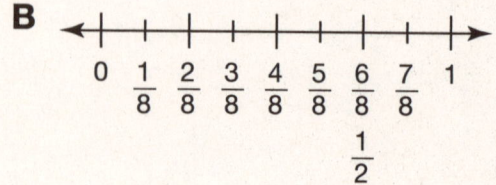

C
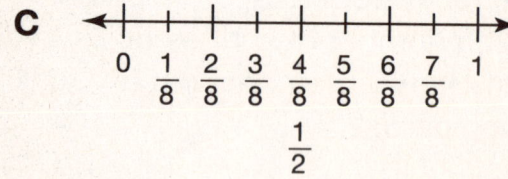

B

D
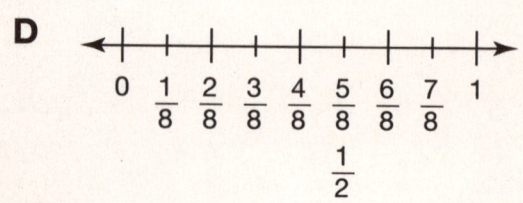

Equivalent Fractions and the Number Line

1. Write two fractions that name the location on the number line below.

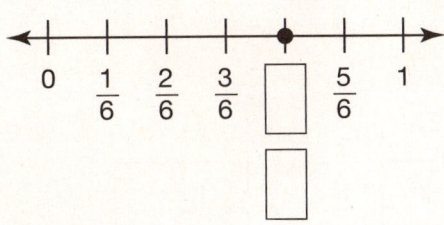

For **2** and **3,** draw a number line to show that the fractions are equivalent.

2. $\frac{3}{4} = \frac{6}{8}$

3. $\frac{1}{4} = \frac{2}{8}$

4. **Reason** Explain how you can use a number line to show that $\frac{3}{6}$ and $\frac{1}{2}$ are equivalent fractions.

_____

_____

_____

_____

Equal parts of a Whole

Length Likeness

Circle the figure that is the same length as the first figure.

1.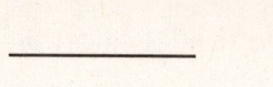

2.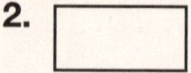

3.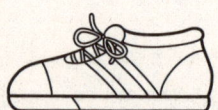

4.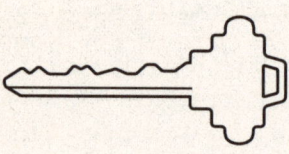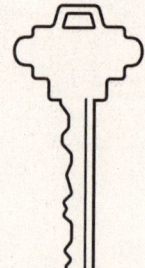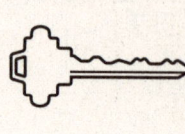

5.

Name _____

Choose the best answer.

1. What is the missing number on the number line below?

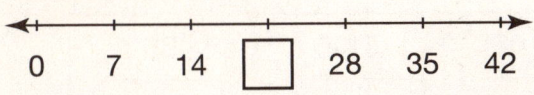

0   7   14   ☐   28   35   42

A 17   C 23

B 21   D 25

2. **Mental Math** Roger's score on a computer game is 989 points. Greg's score is 212 points. How many more points does Roger have than Greg?

A 767   C 787

B 777   D 877

3. Which fraction of the counters are black?

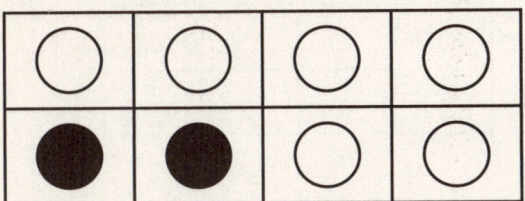

A $\frac{6}{8}$ C $\frac{2}{8}$

B $\frac{4}{8}$ D $\frac{1}{8}$

4. Gil has 6 orange crayons, 4 red crayons, and 5 black crayons. How many crayons does Gil have in all?

_____

5. Write a fact family involving 3, 6, and 18.

_____

_____

_____

6. Jenny made 6 baskets for every two her sister made. If her sister made 6 baskets, how many did Jenny make?

_____

7. Compare. Write <, >, or =.

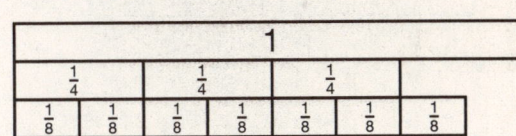

$\frac{3}{4}$ ◯ $\frac{7}{8}$

Whole Numbers and Fractions

Sal ate $\frac{1}{3}$ of a granola bar at breakfast.
He ate another $\frac{1}{3}$ of the bar at lunch. Then he ate $\frac{1}{3}$ of the bar at dinner. How much of the granola bar did he eat in all?

You can use fraction strips to model how much of the granola bar Sal ate.

Count the fraction strips.

Breakfast	Lunch	Dinner
$\frac{1}{3}$	$\frac{1}{3}$	$\frac{1}{3}$

There are three. Sal ate three $\frac{1}{3}$s of a granola bar. You can write this as the fraction $\frac{3}{3}$.

Now, compare the fraction strips to 1 whole.

1		
$\frac{1}{3}$	$\frac{1}{3}$	$\frac{1}{3}$

So, $\frac{3}{3}$ is equal to 1 whole. You can say Sal ate $\frac{3}{3}$ of a granola bar. Or you can say Sal ate 1 granola bar.

For **1** and **2**, count the fraction strips.
Write the fraction name and equivalent whole number name for each.

1.

1			
$\frac{1}{4}$	$\frac{1}{4}$	$\frac{1}{4}$	$\frac{1}{4}$

_____

2.

1		1	
$\frac{1}{2}$	$\frac{1}{2}$	$\frac{1}{2}$	$\frac{1}{2}$

_____

For **3–6,** write an equivalent fraction for each whole number.

3. 3 _____

4. 2 _____

5. 6 _____

6. 4 _____

7. Persevere Jane gets $\frac{1}{2}$ of a gold star each time she helps her teacher clean up the classroom after art class. How many times would Jane need to help her teacher to earn 3 whole gold stars? Draw fraction strips to help.

_____

Whole Numbers and Fractions

In **1–6**, write an equivalent fraction for each whole number.

1. 6   **2.** 8   **3.** 4   **4.** 3   **5.** 1   **6.** 5

_____   _____   _____   _____   _____   _____

7. Reason Explain how you know $\frac{6}{6}$ and 1 are equivalent.

_____

_____

_____

In **8–9**, use the fraction name to divide the number line into equal parts.

8. thirds

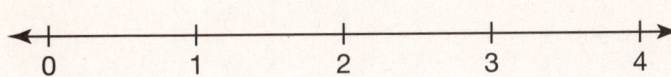

9. fourths

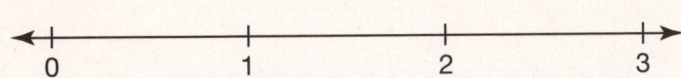

10. Which whole number is equivalent to $\frac{8}{2}$?

A 2   **B** 4   **C** 6   **D** 8

11. Critique Reasoning Molly is wrapping up parts of sandwiches to sell at her sandwich cart. She cuts each sandwich in fourths and then wraps each fourth separately. She says that she wrapped 16 fourths, so she wrapped 16 whole sandwiches. What was Molly's mistake?

_____

_____

_____

_____

Time After Time

JANUARY						
S	M	T	W	T	F	S
		1	2	3	4	5
6	7	8	9	10	11	12
13	14	15	16	17	18	19
20	21	22	23	24	25	26
27	28	29	30	31		

APRIL						
S	M	T	W	T	F	S
		1	2	3	4	5	6
7	8	9	10	11	12	13
14	15	16	17	18	19	20
21	22	23	24	25	26	27
28	29	30				

JULY						
S	M	T	W	T	F	S
	1	2	3	4	5	6
7	8	9	10	11	12	13
14	15	16	17	18	19	20
21	22	23	24	25	26	27
28	29	30	31			

OCTOBER						
S	M	T	W	T	F	S
		1	2	3	4	5
6	7	8	9	10	11	12
13	14	15	16	17	18	19
20	21	22	23	24	25	26
27	28	29	30	31		

Estimate the fraction of each month that passed before the date given.

1. January 8 _____

2. October 17 _____

3. April 16 _____

4. July 5 _____

5. October 10 _____

6. January 25 _____

7. July 6 _____

8. April 30 _____

Name _____

Choose the best answer.

1. **Mental Math** Jack has 32 quarters. He wants to trade them in for dollar bills. Four quarters equal one dollar. How many dollars can Jack get?

   A 4

   B 7

   C 8

   D 9

2. Sam recycles milk bottles. A box will hold 2 rows of 3 milk bottles. Sam has 24 milk bottles. How many boxes does he need to hold all the bottles?

   A 8   **C** 5

   B 6   **D** 4

3. Kirsten goes to school 180 days each year. There have been 105 school days so far this year. How many more school days are there this year?

   A 80

   B 75

   C 70

   D 65

4. Donald made a flag that was $\frac{2}{4}$ black. Which flag is Donald's?

   A    **C**

   B    **D**

5. The picture shows how much of a pan of cornbread was left after dinner. Which fraction describes about how much was left?

   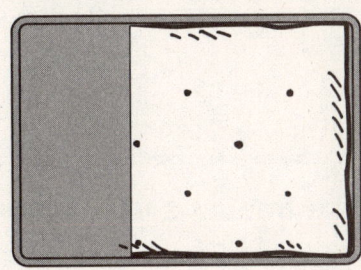

   A $\frac{1}{2}$

   B $\frac{1}{3}$

   C $\frac{2}{3}$

   D $\frac{1}{4}$

Using Fractions

You can use fraction strips or a number line to compare and order fractions and mixed numbers.

Compare $\frac{3}{4}$, $\frac{5}{8}$, and $\frac{1}{2}$. Which fraction is the greatest? the least?

Use fraction strips to compare.

$\frac{1}{4}$	$\frac{1}{4}$	$\frac{1}{4}$		
$\frac{1}{8}$	$\frac{1}{8}$	$\frac{1}{8}$	$\frac{1}{8}$	$\frac{1}{8}$
$\frac{1}{2}$				

$\frac{3}{4} > \frac{5}{8}$ and $\frac{5}{8} > \frac{1}{2}$

$\frac{3}{4}$ is the greatest.

$\frac{1}{2}$ is the least.

Use a number line to compare.

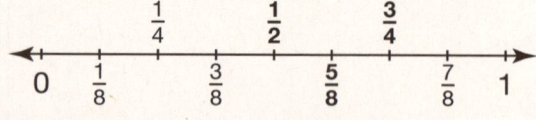

$\frac{3}{4}$ is to the right of $\frac{5}{8}$ so $\frac{3}{4} > \frac{5}{8}$.

$\frac{5}{8}$ is to the right of $\frac{1}{2}$ so $\frac{5}{8} > \frac{1}{2}$.

$\frac{3}{4}$ is the greatest.

$\frac{1}{2}$ is the least.

In **1–4**, write the fractions in order from least to greatest.

1. $\frac{4}{6}, \frac{3}{8}, \frac{1}{2}$ _____

2. $\frac{5}{6}, \frac{3}{4}, \frac{4}{8}$ _____

3. $\frac{1}{2}, \frac{6}{8}, \frac{2}{6}$ _____

4. $\frac{3}{8}, \frac{1}{2}, \frac{1}{4}$ _____

$\frac{1}{2}$				$\frac{1}{2}$			
$\frac{1}{4}$		$\frac{1}{4}$		$\frac{1}{4}$		$\frac{1}{4}$	
$\frac{1}{6}$		$\frac{1}{6}$	$\frac{1}{6}$	$\frac{1}{6}$		$\frac{1}{6}$	$\frac{1}{6}$
$\frac{1}{8}$	$\frac{1}{8}$	$\frac{1}{8}$	$\frac{1}{8}$	$\frac{1}{8}$	$\frac{1}{8}$	$\frac{1}{8}$	$\frac{1}{8}$

In **5–8**, use the number line to compare. Write $<$, $>$, or $=$.

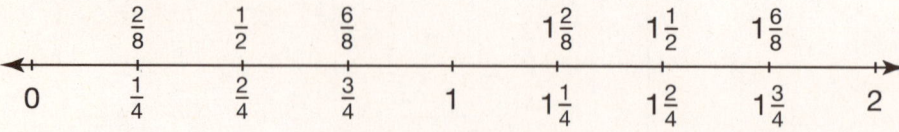

5. $\frac{2}{4} \bigcirc \frac{1}{2}$ **6.** $1\frac{1}{4} \bigcirc 1\frac{6}{8}$ **7.** $\frac{3}{4} \bigcirc 1\frac{3}{4}$ **8.** $\frac{2}{4} \bigcirc \frac{2}{8}$

9. Compare $\frac{3}{4}$ and $\frac{3}{6}$. Without using fraction strips or a number line, how can you tell which fraction is greater?

_____

_____

Name _____

Using Fractions

In **1–6**, compare. Write <, >, or =.

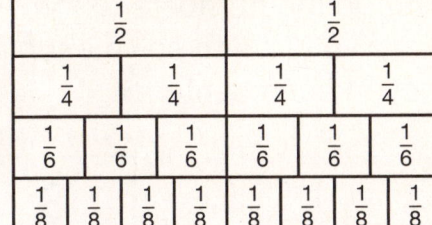

1. $\frac{6}{8}$ ◯ $\frac{1}{2}$ **2.** $\frac{2}{4}$ ◯ $\frac{3}{6}$ **3.** $\frac{2}{8}$ ◯ $\frac{2}{6}$

4. $\frac{1}{2}$ ◯ $\frac{2}{6}$ **5.** $\frac{3}{4}$ ◯ $\frac{3}{8}$ **6.** $\frac{1}{4}$ ◯ $\frac{3}{8}$

7. Complete the number line by writing the missing fractions and mixed numbers.

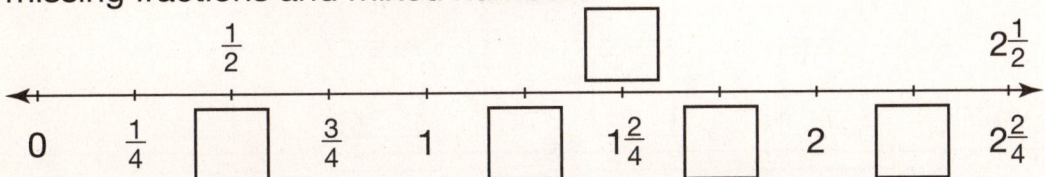

8. About how much of this glass is filled?

A $\frac{1}{3}$

B $\frac{3}{4}$

C $\frac{1}{2}$

D $\frac{1}{8}$

9. Which fraction describes the part of this blanket that is white?

A $\frac{2}{3}$

B $\frac{1}{2}$

C $\frac{2}{4}$

D $\frac{2}{8}$

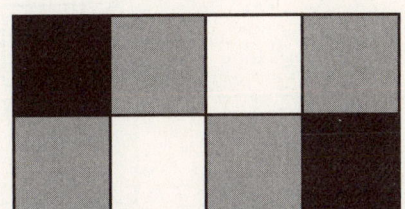

In **10–13**, name the fruit with the greater number of cups in the recipe at the right.

10. Apples or bananas? _____

11. Grapes or coconut? _____

12. Raisins or cherries? _____

13. Apples or pineapple? _____

Fruit Salad
1 batch

$1\frac{1}{2}$ cups apples
$1\frac{3}{4}$ cups grapes
$\frac{1}{2}$ cup raisins
$2\frac{2}{4}$ cups bananas
$\frac{3}{4}$ cup coconut
$1\frac{2}{4}$ cups cherries
$2\frac{1}{4}$ cups pineapple

14. One batch of fruit salad has equal amounts of which kinds of fruit? Explain how you decided.

_____

_____

Puzzling Fractions

Arrange the numbers to form equivalent fractions.
Find two ways to solve each puzzle. Use each number
once in each sentence.

1.

| 8 | 2 | 1 | 4 |

$$\frac{\square}{\square} = \frac{\square}{\square} \qquad \frac{\square}{\square} = \frac{\square}{\square}$$

2.

| 1 | 6 | 3 | 2 |

$$\frac{\square}{\square} = \frac{\square}{\square} \qquad \frac{\square}{\square} = \frac{\square}{\square}$$

3.

| 6 | 8 | 4 | 3 |

$$\frac{\square}{\square} = \frac{\square}{\square} \qquad \frac{\square}{\square} = \frac{\square}{\square}$$

4.

| 3 | 4 | 2 | 6 |

$$\frac{\square}{\square} = \frac{\square}{\square} \qquad \frac{\square}{\square} = \frac{\square}{\square}$$

Choose the best answer.

1. What fraction of the circles are shaded?

 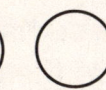

A $\frac{1}{3}$

B $\frac{1}{4}$

C $\frac{3}{1}$

D $\frac{3}{4}$

2. Which is closest to $\frac{7}{8}$ on a number line?

A 0

B $\frac{3}{8}$

C $\frac{5}{8}$

D 1

3. Estimation Jenny scored 28 points on one assignment and 32 points on another assignment. About how many points has Jenny scored on the two assignments?

A 60

B 50

C 40

D 30

4. Wendy made the octagon below.

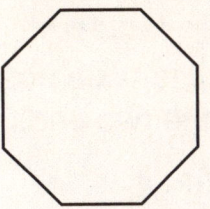

How many sides does the octagon have?

A 4

B 6

C 8

D 10

5. One year 490,513 people attended the Florida State Fair.

a. Write the number 490,513 in expanded form.

_____

_____

b. Which digit is in the ten thousands place?

_____

Problem Solving: Draw a Picture

A fence is 20 feet long. It has a post at each end. The fence also has a post every 4 feet between the two ends. How many fence posts are there in all?

Read and Understand

Step 1   What do you know?

The fence is 20 feet long.
A fence post is at each end.
There is a fence post every 4 feet.

Step 2   What are you trying to find?

How many posts the fence has

Plan and Solve

Step 3   What strategy will you use?   **Strategy:** Draw a picture

| 4 feet | 4 feet | 4 feet | 4 feet | 4 feet |

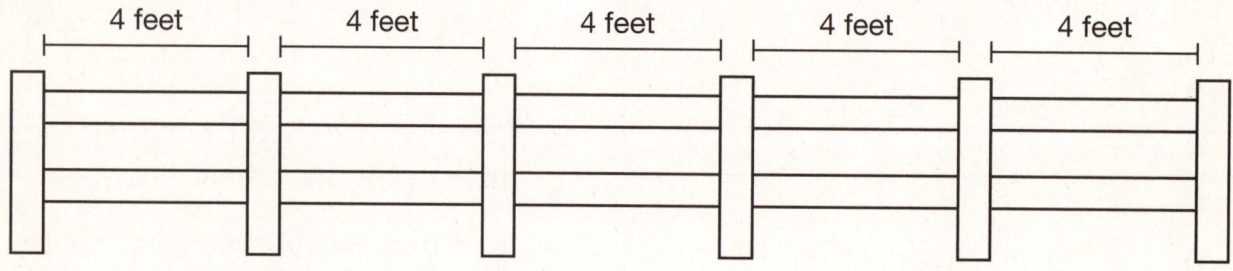

There are 6 fence posts in all.

Look Back and Check

Step 4   Is your work correct?

Yes, the picture shows a fence that is 20 feet long. It has a fence post at each end, and a fence post every 4 feet. There are 6 fence posts.

Solve. Draw a picture.

1. Jamie put 8 squares together to make a rectangle. There are 2 rows of squares. Each row has 4 squares. How many pairs of sides touch each other in the rectangle?

2. Trent, Linda, and Pam will work together to paint a poster that is 4 feet long. Each student will paint an equal length of the poster. How many feet of the poster length will each student paint?

Problem Solving: Draw a Picture

Solve. Draw a picture.

1. Larry used a pattern of colors to make a cube train. He used
a red cube, a blue cube, a red cube, and another red cube
before he started the pattern again. He used 15 cubes.
How many red cubes did Larry use?

_____

2. Two pizzas were each cut into sixths. Ashraf, Drew,
and Katie shared the pizzas equally. How many
sixths did each friend get?

_____

3. Eric and Frank want to equally share $\frac{4}{3}$ feet of rope. What
length of rope should each friend get? Explain how to use a
drawing to help solve the problem.

_____

_____

_____

4. A square garden is 12 feet long on each side. Janet needs to
put a post at each corner. She also needs to put a post every
3 feet on each side. How many posts does Janet need?

A 12   **B** 16   **C** 20   **D** 24

Picture Patterns

Use the pictures to find a pattern. Then complete the table.

1.

A   B   C

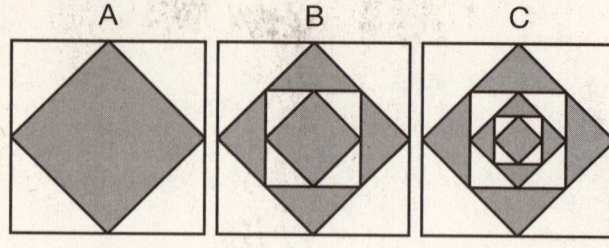

Figure	A	B	C	D
Number of Squares	2	4	6	
Fraction of Shaded Squares	$\frac{1}{2}$	$\frac{2}{4}$		

2.

A   B   C

Carton Stack	A	B	C	D
Number of Cartons	1	3	9	
Fraction Representing One Carton	1	$\frac{1}{3}$		

3.

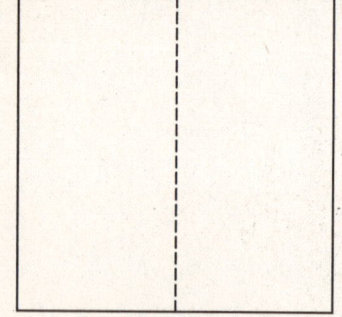 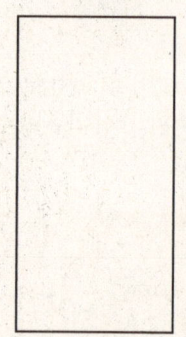 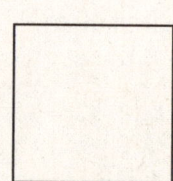 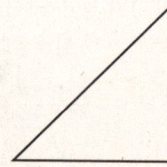 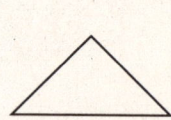

Square piece of paper   1 fold   2 folds   3 folds   4 folds

Number of Folds	1	2	3	4
Number of Parts	2	4	8	
Fraction Representing One Part	$\frac{1}{2}$	$\frac{1}{4}$		